Mel Bay Presents The Frank Vignola Jazz Play

Jazz Solos
Improvised Solos over Standard Progressions
Volume 1
by Frank Vignola

CD CONTENTS

1	All the Things You're Not [2:37]		6	Scrapple the Green Apples [2:02]
2	What's Up with this Thing Called Love [2:47]		7	I Did Remember April [3:07]
3	Blue Dolphin Street [3:02]		8	Girls from Ipanema-ville [3:25]
4	Taking the B Train [2:34]		9	Impressionistic [1:53]
5	Satin Dolls [3:03]		10	Dorian Ideas [2:30]

1 2 3 4 5 6 7 8 9 0

Visit us on the Web at www.melbay.com — E-mail us at email@melbay.com

Contents

Play these solos in other positions besides the one indicated in TAB. To do so, simply find the starting note in another area of the fingerboard and figure out the solo in that position. You can also use each of your four fingers as starting points to find other ways to play these etudes.

ALL THE THINGS YOU'RE NOT
(Track #1)

FRANK VIGNOLA

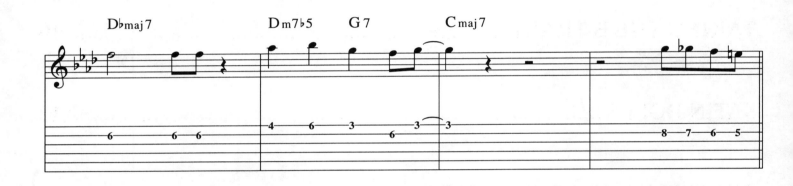

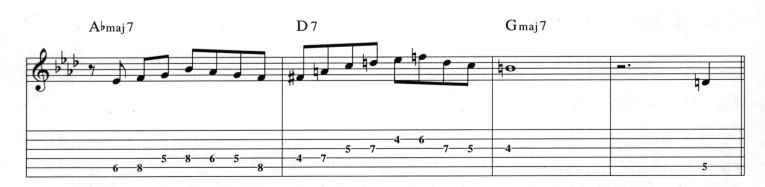

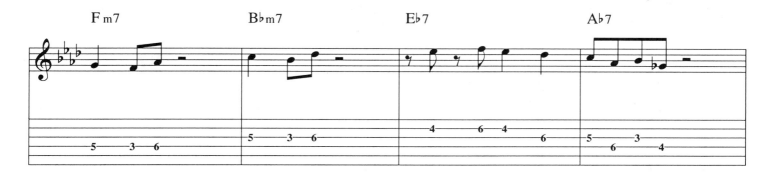

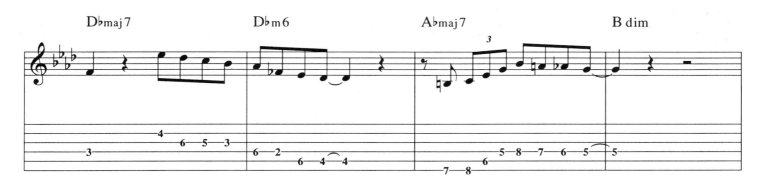

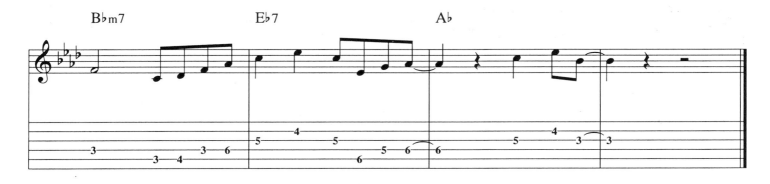

WHAT'S UP WITH THIS THING CALLED LOVE?
(Track #2)

FRANK VIGNOLA

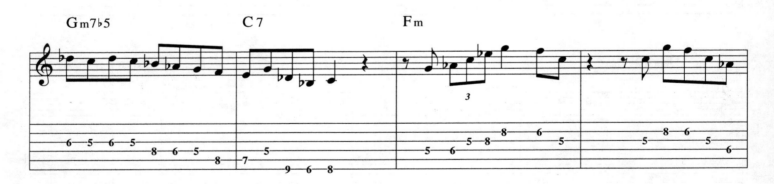

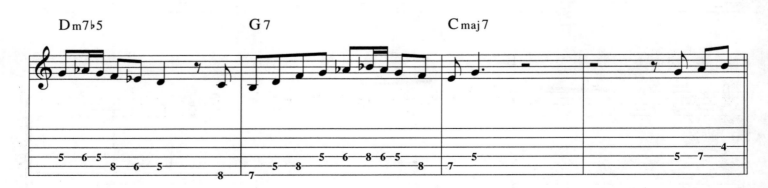

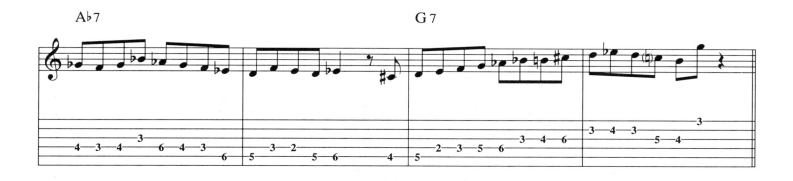

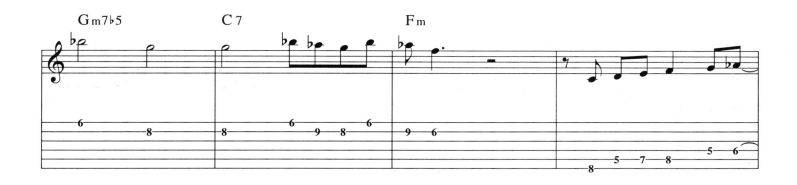

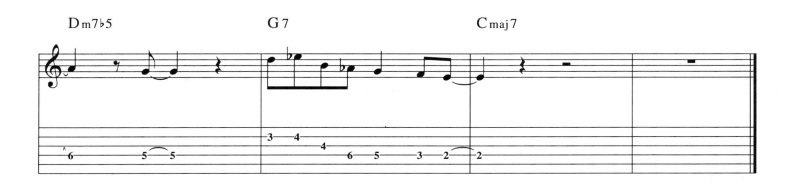

7

BLUE DOLPHIN STREET
(Track #3)

FRANK VIGNOLA

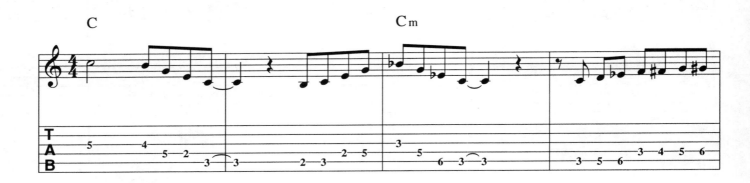

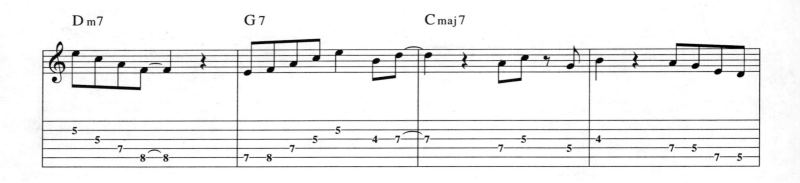

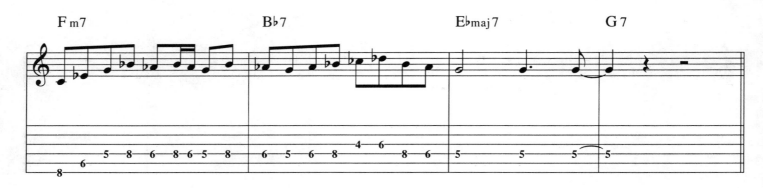

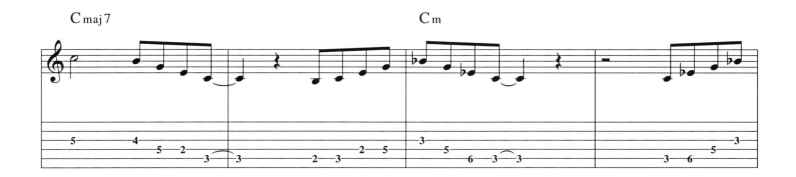

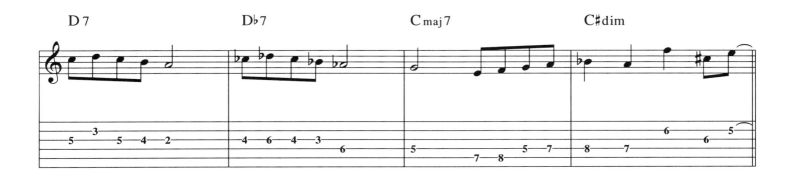

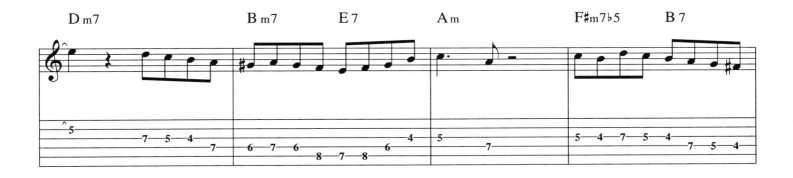

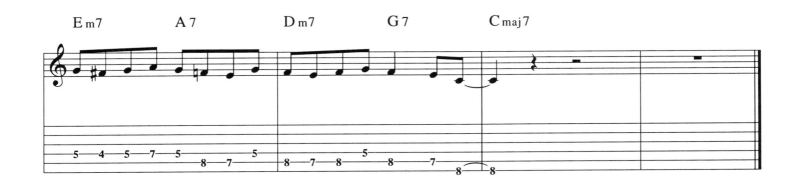

TAKING THE B TRAIN
(Track #4)

FRANK VIGNOLA

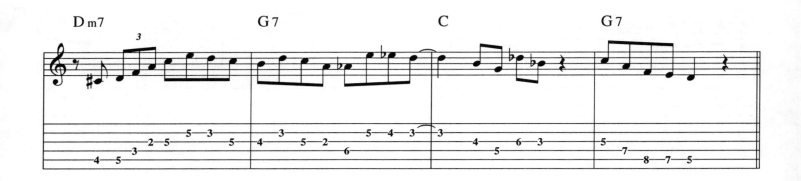

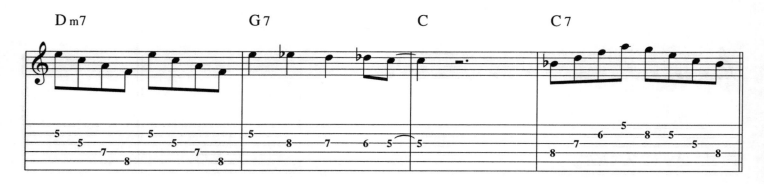

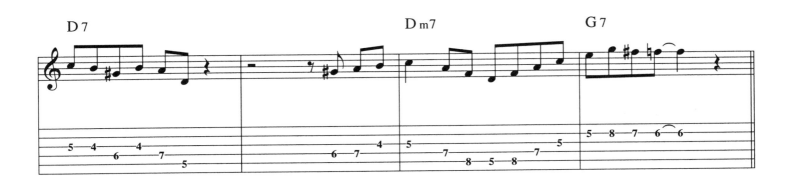

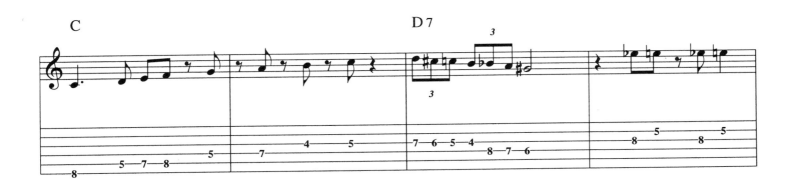

SATIN DOLLS
(Track #5)

FRANK VIGNOLA

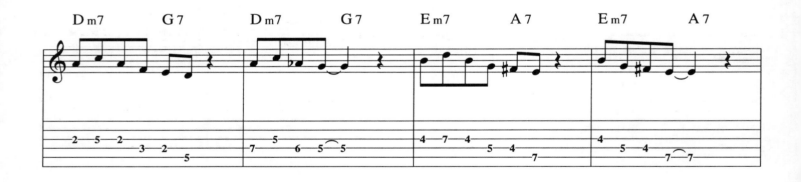

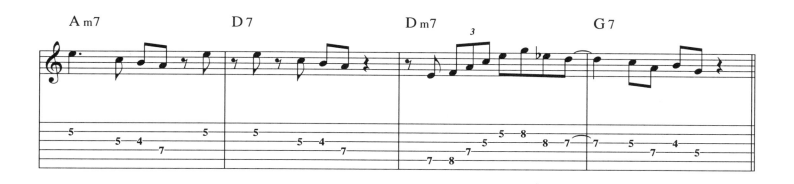

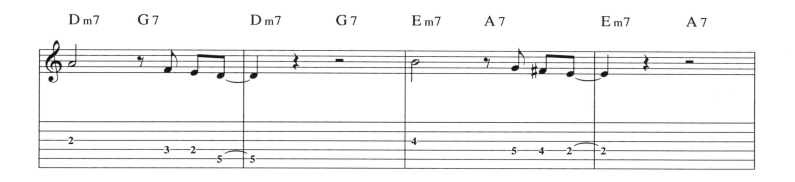

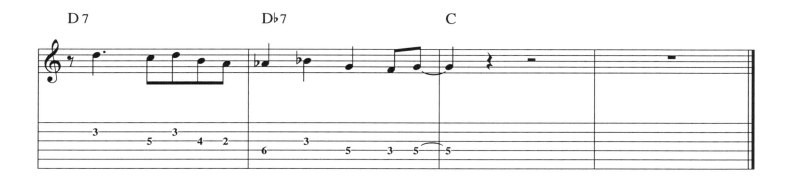

SCRAPPLE THE GREEN APPLES
(Track #6)

FRANK VIGNOLA

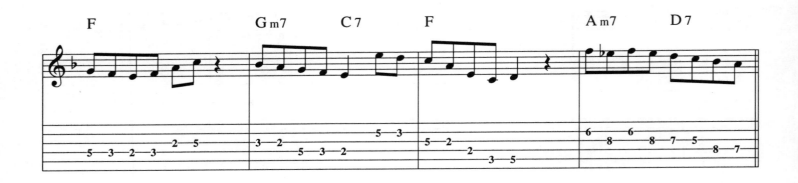

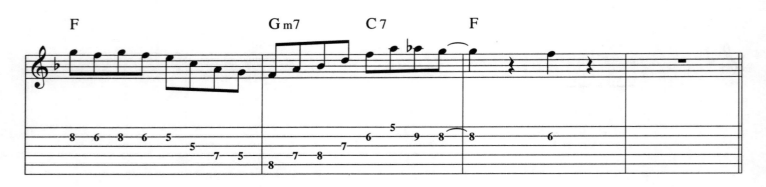

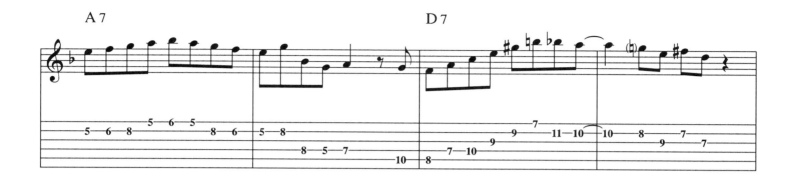
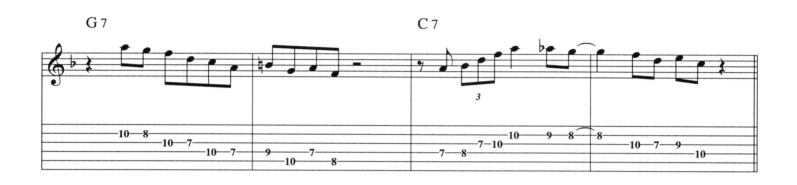
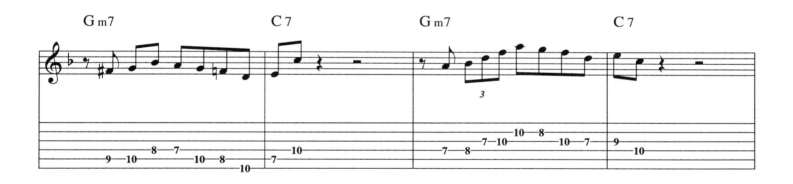
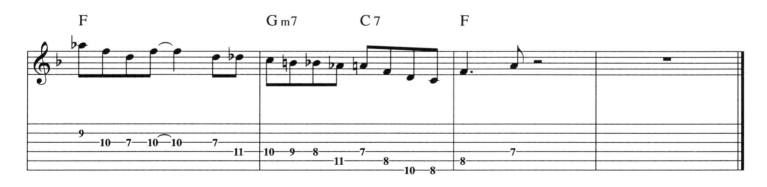

15

I DID REMEMBER APRIL
(Track #7)

FRANK VIGNOLA

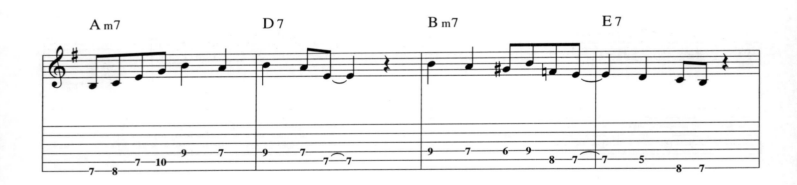

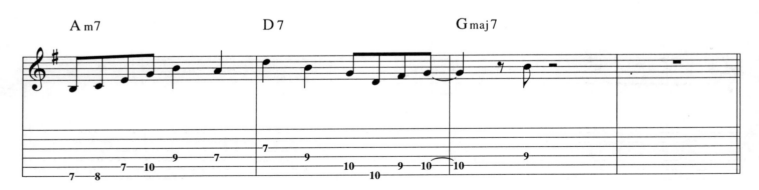

16

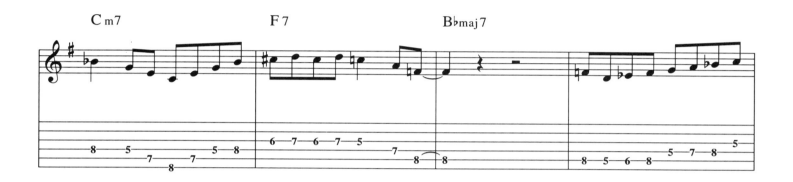

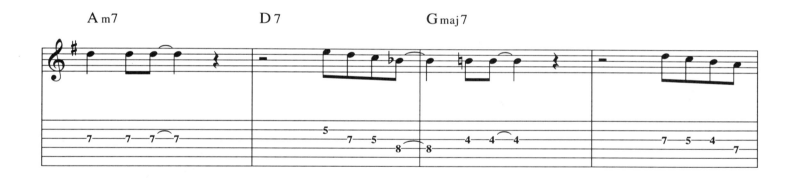

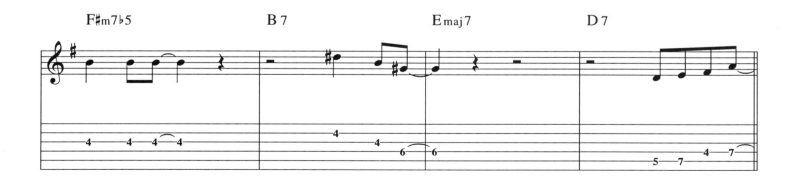

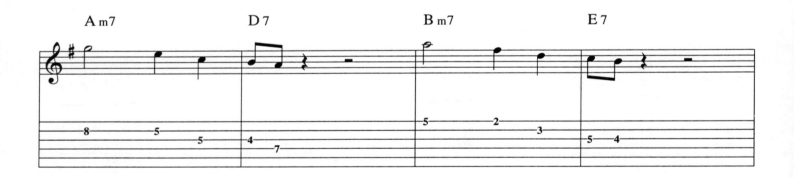

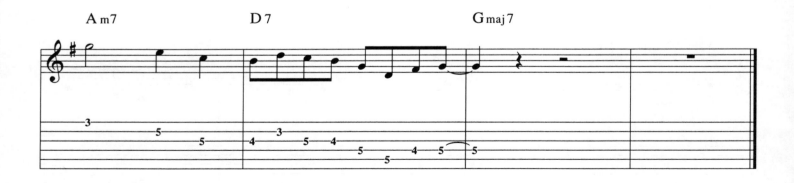

GIRLS FROM IPANEMA-VILLE
(Track #8)

FRANK VIGNOLA

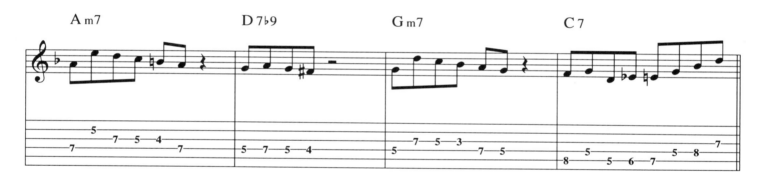

21

IMPRESSIONISTIC
(Track #9)

FRANK VIGNOLA

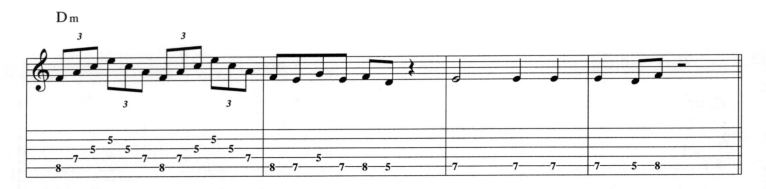

22

E♭m

E♭m

Dm

Dm

DORIAN IDEAS
(Track #10)

FRANK VIGNOLA

FRANK VIGNOLA

Frank Vignola is considered to be among the top rank of guitarists on the music scene today. Born on December 30, 1965, in Long Island, New York, he began playing guitar at the age of five. As his proficiency grew, he spent many hours listening to the music of legendary guitarists, Django Reinhardt, Joe Pass, and Johnny Smith. Frank not only gained a spiritual sort of inspiration from these guitarists recordings, he also made an intricate study of the complexities of these guitar masters styles, slowing down his records to analyze many a solo.

Frank's first teacher was his father, a semi-professional banjo player. Later, Frank became the star pupil of guitarist Jimmy George, who was one of the original Dion and the Belmonts. At age 12, Frank took up the tenor banjo and swiftly burst upon the music scene in a way that would portend many of the accolades and milestones to come in his career as a jazz guitarist.

Though obviously steeped in the traditional schools of jazz, especially in the formative years, Frank would ultimately take inspiration from a wide arc of the musical spectrum. Guitarists such as Django, Charlie Christian, Wes Montgomery and Lonnie Johnson are obvious influences, but one might be surprised to learn that rocker Jimi Hendrix has also received the close scrutiny of Frank's ear. Louis Armstrong, Lester Young, Thelonius Monk, Charlie Parker, Sonny Stitt, Antonio Carlos Jobim, Thad Jones and Duke Ellington have all had inspirational impact on the music of Frank Vignola.

While still in his teens, Frank experienced the most effective music education possible—right on the bandstand as a working musician. Soon named among the top ranked musicians in New York, Frank performed and toured with such headliners as Max Morath and Leon Redbone. At age 23, he decided to lead his own group and formed his version of the famed Quintet of the Hot Club of France. Their debut at the New York cabaret, Michael's Pub, was a smash success and launched his career as a guitarist 'in the spotlight.' Tours of Europe, recording sessions, and an exclusive recording contract with the Concord Jazz label would all follow in short succession in a few short years. Frank would perform and/or record with such varied artists as Chet Atkins, Madonna, Jon Faddis, Woody Allen, Ringo Starr, Manhattan Transfer, Frank Wess, Elvin Jones, Lionel Hampton and countless legends from the golden age of jazz.

Currently, Frank Vignola is the guitarist with the Mark O Conner Trio's tribute to Stephane Grappelli and also performs every Monday night with the Les Paul Trio at the Iridium in New York City. Frank is also the new guitarist in John Lewis' new group Evolution.

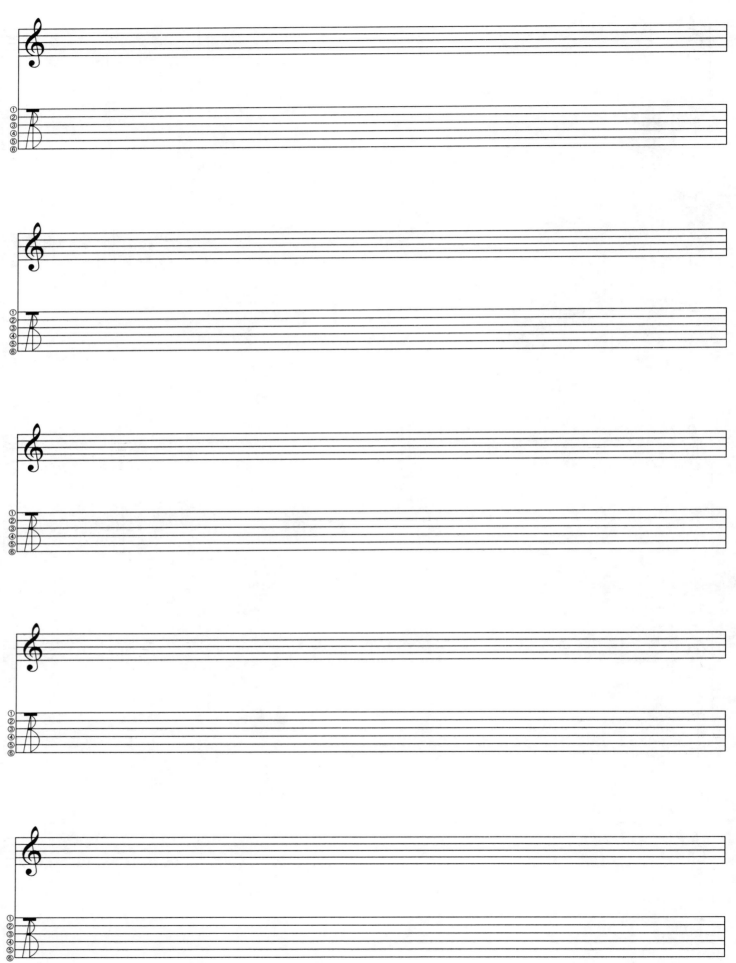

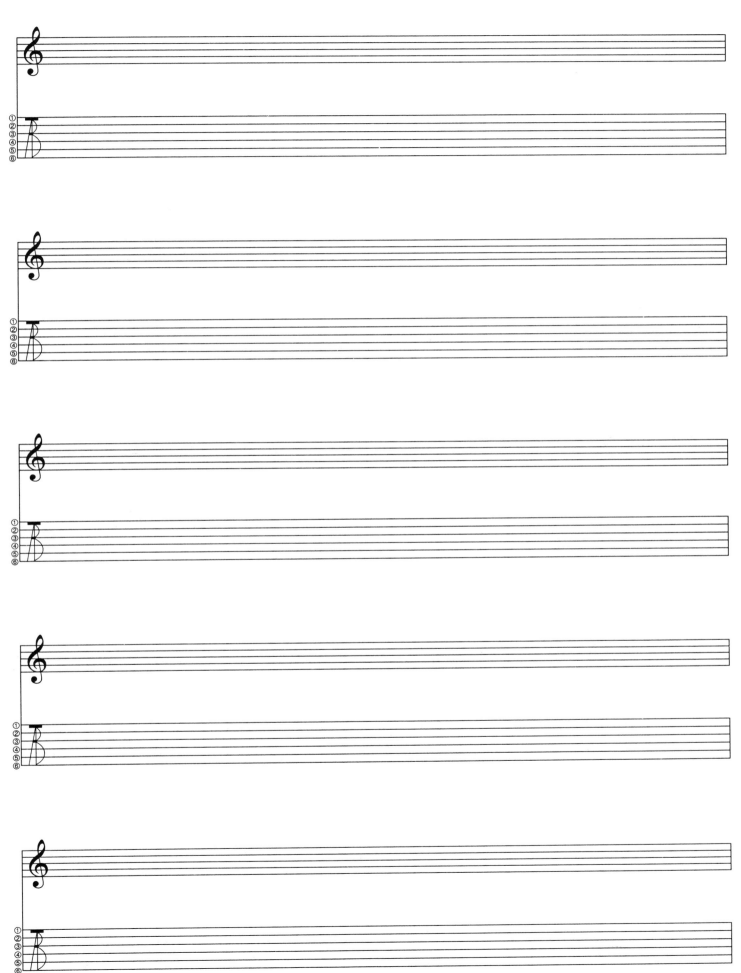

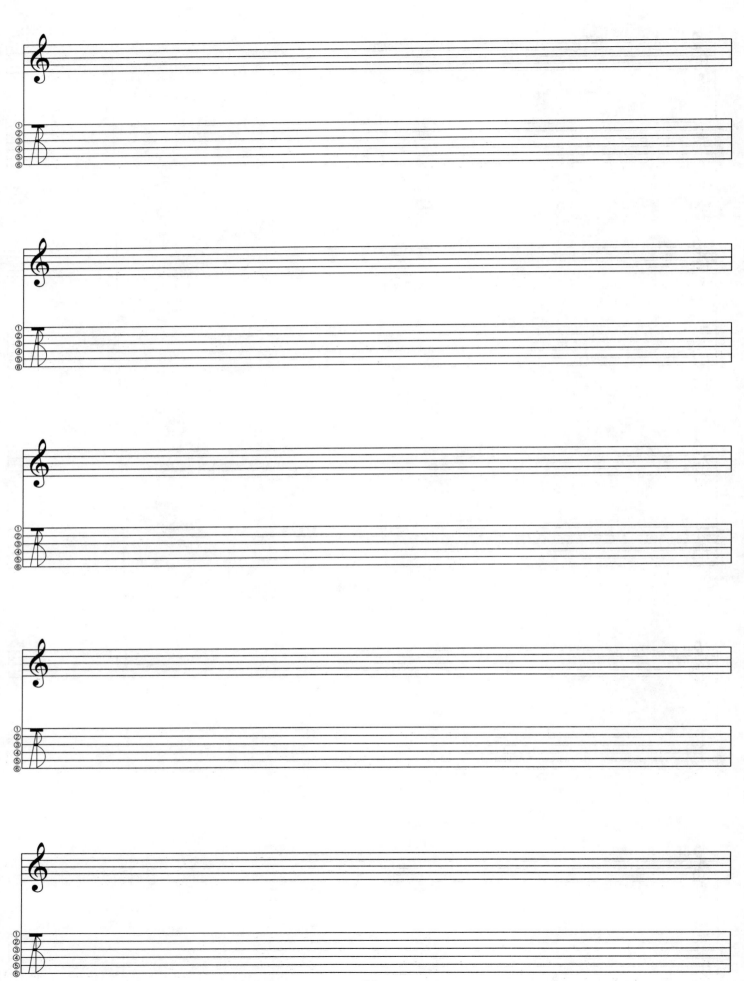

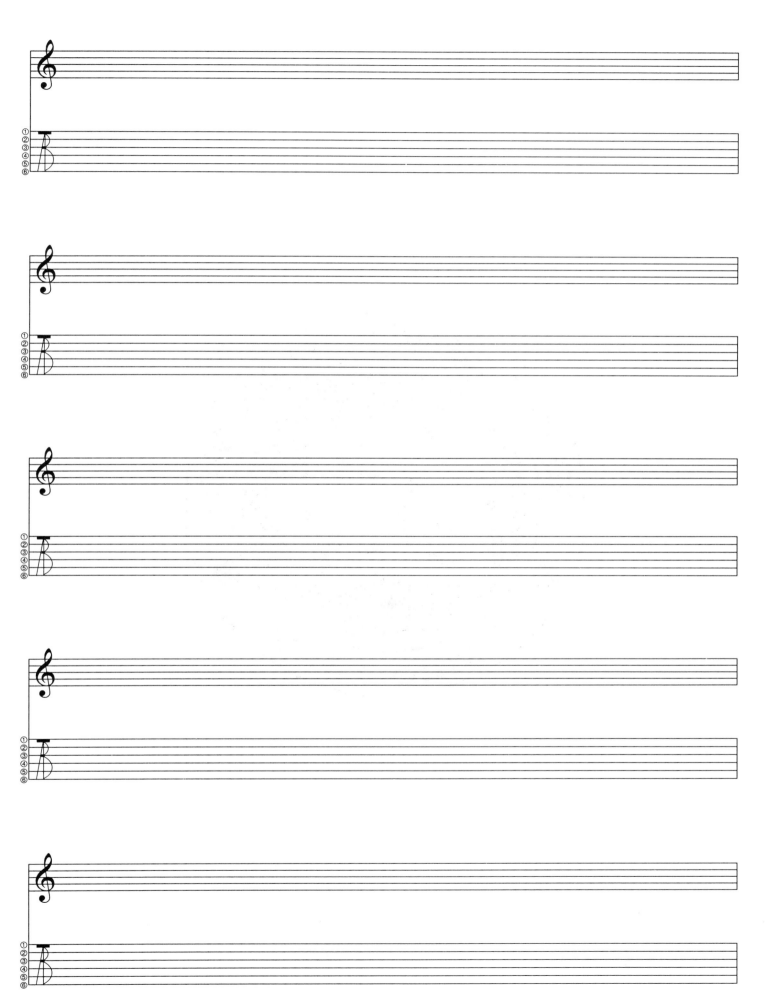